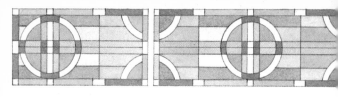

TO A VERY SPECIAL® IS A REGISTERED TRADE MARK OF
EXLEY PUBLICATIONS LTD AND EXLEY GIFTBOOKS.

Other giftbooks by Exley:
Mother Quotations
An Illustrated Mother's Notebook
To a very Special Mother
For Mother, A Gift of Love
To The World's Best Mother
The Best of Women's Quotations
The Love Between Mothers and Sons
The Love Between Mothers and Daughters
Women's Thoughts
In Celebration of Women

Published simultaneously in 1997 by Exley Giftbooks in the USA and
Exley Publications Ltd in Great Britain.

12 11 10 9 8 7 6 5 4 3 2 1
Copyright © Helen Exley 1997
ISBN 1-85015-840-1

Edited by Helen Exley.
Written by Pam Brown.
Illustrated by Judith O'Dwyer.
Printed and bound in Hungary.

Exley Publications Ltd, 16 Chalk Hill, Watford, Herts WD1 4BN, UK.
Exley Giftbooks, 232 Madison Avenue, Suite 1206, NY 10016, USA.

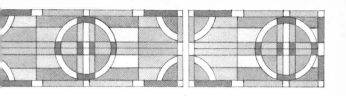

THANK YOU
TO A VERY SPECIAL
Mother

A HELEN EXLEY GIFTBOOK

Written by Pam Brown
Illustrations by Judith O'Dwyer
Edited by Helen Exley

EXLEY
NEW YORK • WATFORD, UK

THANK YOU FOR MY CHILDHOOD, FOR MY LIFE

Thank you for giving me life – for the chance to watch great waves breaking along the shore, to hear the shout of bird-song in the dawn, to hold my hands beneath running water, to smell grass after rain, to taste fresh bread. For the gifts of friendship, laughter and creativity.

–

You created the scent of childhood – hot strawberry jelly, new bread, coal tar soap, geraniums, clean sheets, lavender talc, floor polish, toffee. Thank you.

–

Thank you for giving me a childhood on which I could build a life.

–

*E*veryone needs a mother to cheer when things go right.

It's good to have the applause of lovers, friends, husbands and colleagues – but one looks above their heads, to make sure Mum is clapping!

—

*T*hank you for keeping me safe within yourself so long, sheltering me in my most secret life, releasing me at last to independence. Giving me welcome, teaching me love. Caring for me through sickness, tears, tantrums and stubborn, sullen silences. Believing in me – even at the edges of despair.

—

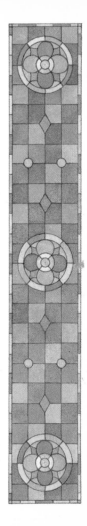

THE CERTAINTY OF
YOUR LOVE

Mothers endure every illness, every grief, every
anxiety suffered by their children – often powerless
to help. Only able to wait, to love.
Thank you – for that love is what I hold on to.

—

You did make the most awful mistakes at times.
No doubt the psychologists would wince.
But you loved me. Love me.
And I love you back.
So "boo" to the psychologists.
We know more than they do.
Thank you for being my dear mother.

—

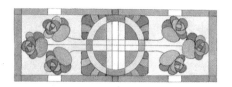

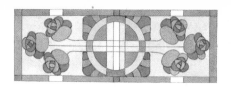

There's no such thing as the archetypal Mother save in the purely biological sense. There are as many sorts of mother as there are women. Gentle, ferocious, brainy, dim, somnolent, hyperactive, smiling, grim. Disciplinarians or prone to laissez-faire. Ambitious and driving, or accepting the fact that their happy, smiling piglets will never learn to fly.

Some destroy. But most, in one fashion or another, raise their children and send them on their way with the best gift that anyone can give. The certainty of love.

—

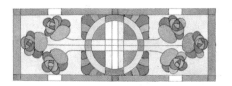

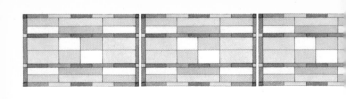

Mothers look at their newborn babies with
awe – so small, so dependent, so packed
with secrets and possibilities. But they are
sure that love will see them through.
And it does.
Though through joys and troubles beyond
their imagining.
Somehow they find strength and wisdom
they never knew they possessed.
Somehow they become, quietly and
unobtrusively, the keystones of our lives.
This is to thank them all for all their
courage, patience, kindness, understanding.
This is to thank you, the most loving of
mothers, especially.

—

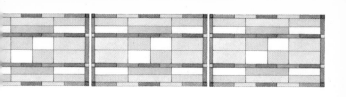

Thank you for fitting your life to ours.

Thank you for making us feel that

nothing that you have achieved is worth

more than our love.

Thank you for making us feel wanted,

precious, irreplaceable.

Thank you for being you.

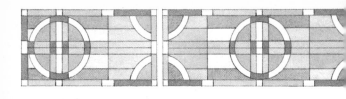

YOU'VE ALWAYS BEEN THERE FOR ME

Mothers are people who stay up till midnight to get a shepherd's dress made from a bath towel by morning. Because the shepherd had forgotten to mention the Nativity Play till the night before.
Thanks Mum.

–

A kinder god would have seen that mothers sprouted extra sets of arms with every birth.

–

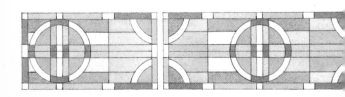

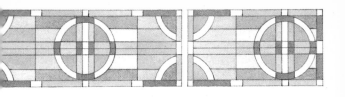

If needs be you will come from the ends of the world at half an hour's notice. Or hop on a bus.
Thank you for being there come fire,
flood or penury.
Thank you for being ready to lend anything, give anything that will help us through.
Thank you for always being ready to help.

—

Thank you for the sleepless nights, the anxious days and the financial nightmares that were part and parcel of my childhood.
But about which I knew nothing – I only knew the happiness of your love and the certainty of your care.

—

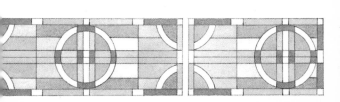

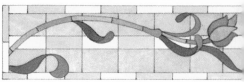

THANK YOU FOR A LIFETIME OF LITTLE THINGS

*And thank you for the little things, the
ordinary things I took for granted; trivial
when seen day by day, but mounting up
to mind-boggling statistics over those
years of childhood.
The meals. Hundreds of them. Thousands
of them. Enough to make Gargantua
blanch. An Everest of crockery and glass.
The laundry basket that filled as it was
emptied – like a fairy tale.
The insatiable Charybdis that swirled the
socks and shirts.*

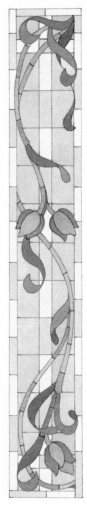

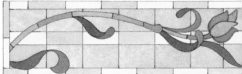

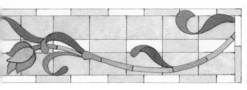

Floors – endless Steppes over which we
tracked sand and mud and bike oil as soon
as they were clean.
And if we remembered, just now and
again, to put our sports gear in the basket,
or dried a few plates, or ran over to the
shop for half a pound of margarine – how
virtuous we felt.
And how delighted you were.
Dearest Mum – it's a bit late in the day.
But go and sit down.
I'll make the tea.

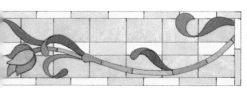

YOU BELIEVE IN ME

FRAZZLED NERVES,
SLEEPLESS NIGHTS, SPOILED DINNERS,
PLANS DESTROYED, WORN CARPETS,
SCUFFED FURNITURE, BLOCKED DRAINS,
TRODDEN FLOWER BEDS. ALL THE
DISAPPOINTMENTS AND DISASTERS, LARGE
AND SMALL, I'VE SCATTERED IN MY WAKE.
THANK YOU FOR FORGIVING ME. THANK
YOU FOR MAKING ME SURE AND CERTAIN
THAT FOR YOU A CHILD OUTWEIGHS ANY
POSSESSION, HOWEVER TREASURED.

—

YOU HAVE BEEN THE LIGHT
AT THE END OF THE TUNNEL, THE HAND-
HOLD ON THE CLIFF FACE, THE PATH
THROUGH THE THICKET. YOU HAVE BEEN
CERTAINTY WHEN ALL SEEMED CHAOS.

—

You put up with me through all the Nothing Days – when nothing made sense, nothing was worth bothering about.

You went on believing that one day I'd come out of the fog and find the sun again.

And I did.

–

Thank you for monumental scoldings, volcanic wrath, reproaches that wrung my heart. Delivered on the spot – with no dire promises of punishment to come. Over. Done with. Sorrow accepted. Arms opened wide. Hugs. And peace restored.

–

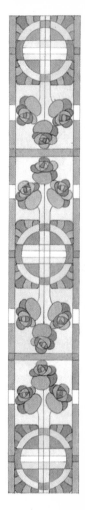

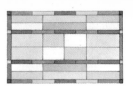

FORGIVING ME

*Thank you for going on loving me
when I was most unlovable.
For believing in me when I no longer
believed in myself.
For helping me to accept
myself as I am
and to be glad to be alive.*

—

*Thank you for forgiving me when
what I had done was just about
unforgivable.*

—

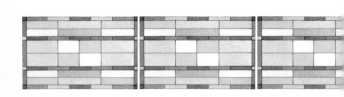

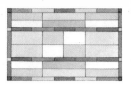

You think I do not see. You seem
always so strong, so sure, so confident
that I will come through. But I know
how often you have lain awake, living
through everything we suffer. I know
it is the burden every dearly loved
child lays upon its mother – without
intention, without any means of
alleviation. "Thank you" is so
inadequate. But it is all I can
find to say.
And that I love you.

—

THROUGH THE LOW TIMES

Thank you for putting up with temper, defiance, laziness, contrariness. Spite. Noise and untidiness. Stupidity and showings-off. All the battery of awfulness a child employs to see how far it is allowed to go. You stood your ground. You went on loving me.

How, I am not too sure.
But thanks.

—

Children pillage their mothers' lives – taking whatever they require – as if by right. It is only later that they come to realize that mothers too have dreams.

—

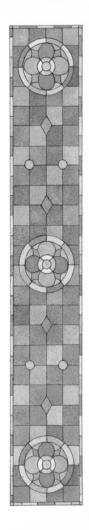

Mothers and children,
however much they love each other, can
hurt each other bitterly. A sudden flash of
temper or frustration, an unconsidered
judgement, a piece of blind ingratitude can
scar the heart. If I could call back the
unkindness and stupidity, the lack of
understanding I have shown you over the
years, I would.

But life is kind, if love is there.
It dulls those cruel hurts – and teaches us
that we are only human, you and I.

I love you exactly as you are.
I would not have you any other way.

—

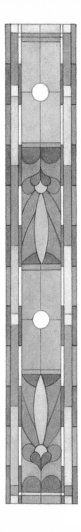

A CERTAIN MAGIC!

You made even the rock-bottom days
exciting – standing before the near empty
larder and saying "Now – what can we
make from this?".
An egg meant pancakes.
No egg meant scones.
"Let's go and hunt for blackberries" meant
crumble, pie, a latticed tart and fool.

–

*T*hank you for always being ready to hop,
skip, jump, throw, catch, climb, model,
draw, sing, shout and applaud.
It made all the difference. It made
childhood a happy place to be.

–

*T*hank you for ignoring all the statistics of failure and saying "Poof! We'll manage!". And we did.

—

*S*ensible mothers let their children sleep. Mothers like you take them out of bed to see a shower of falling stars. Thanks!

—

KEEPING THE FAMILY TOGETHER

Thank you for being at the very heart of the family, holding us together, keeping our concern and affection for one another alive and strong, reminding us of birthdays, tipping us off to one another's needs. Never interfering – but always being there for every one of us.

Whether we need the address of a good plumber, your recipe for lardy cake, advice on the riddance of green fly, or the date of the Battle of Waterloo, whether we are jubilant or in floods of tears, whether we have sensational news or spots, whether we need a hug or the name of a reliable solicitor.

Or simply the answer to 5 across.

—

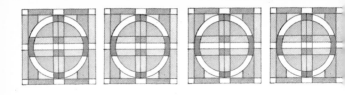

COMFORT

It's strange. Mothers chat with you on the telephone and laugh and gossip — but if you tell them something is most terribly wrong, suddenly they are there with you in the room.
There may be a hundred miles between you, but their arms are round your shoulders.
And what seemed shapeless and overwhelming is made clear — something you can deal with.

—

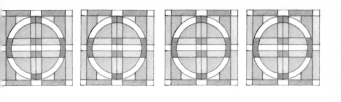

THANK YOU FOR KISSING THINGS BETTER.

–

THANK YOU FOR COMFORT – IN ILLNESS, IN
SORROW, IN ANXIETY, IN DISAPPOINTMENT.
A WOOLLEN SHAWL. A BOWL OF BREAD AND
MILK. A BOX OF FLOWERED TISSUES. YOUR BATH
SALTS. "PETER PAN". A BAG OF JELLY
BEANS. A ROSE-PINK HYACINTH. A TEDDY BEAR
HOT WATER BOTTLE. A DAB OF SCENT.
A PLATE OF BUTTERED TOAST.
AN ARM ABOUT MY SHOULDERS.
THEN. NOW. ALWAYS.

–

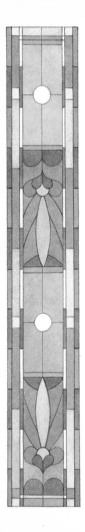

THANK YOU FOR
THOSE YEARS

"See", you said "not one
grass blade is like the other. Value
everything – for it will never come again."
And I have remembered.

–

The years you have given us
are part of me. If I have thought or made
or done new things, they are rooted in what
you taught me.
Thank you for those years.

–

*Thank you for telling me
what I already knew in my heart, but
calmly, clearly, positively.*

So that I could take it from there.

—

*Safe in your arms I found
the moon and stars, sunlight and rain,
bird-song and the sighing of the leaves.*

*Your hands held mine until I could
walk alone. You taught me freedom – and
when the time had come you let me go.*

*Thank you for all that you have given
me. The gifts of life, of love, of laughter.*

—

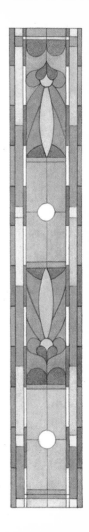